# STEWARDSHIP OF TIME

## STAN TOLER

Copyright 1998
by Beacon Hill Press of Kansas City

ISBN 083-411-7479

Printed in the
United States of America

Cover Design: Ted Ferguson

10  9  8  7  6  5  4  3  2  1

# FOREWORD

This book is the second in the Stewardship Starters series by Stan Toler. This one is designed to help pastors and lay leaders in the Christian management of that most precious commodity—time. Every person on the face of the earth has only 24 hours in a day. What we do with those hours speaks loudly about our relationship with God and others.

Stan Toler has a rare gift for gathering unique quotes and anecdotes that encourage the reader to make better use of this most precious commodity. Stan is a pastor, a teacher, and a businessman who has learned the secrets of using time well. This book is his gift to us who want to better utilize the time we have for the glory of God.

Steve Weber
Director
Stewardship Development Ministries
Church of the Nazarene

# INTRODUCTION

Recently two men from my beloved native state of West Virginia stopped for a visit at Oklahoma City Trinity Church of the Nazarene, where I pastor. These gentlemen were looking for the previous pastor who, coincidentally, was also from West Virginia. After I explained that my predecessor had moved to Phoenix almost 18 months earlier, the driver of the car shook his head. "Fred, I've been late a lot of times in my life," he said to his friend, "But never a year and a half late!" Then he turned to me and said, "How long will it take to get to Phoenix from here?"

"Probably about a year and a half," I joked.

Reflecting on the incident, I laughed. But my laughter turned to sadness as I thought of how some people are always late because they have not learned to be good stewards of time.

While this book will not change habitual tardiness, it does contain guidance, insights, and wisdom to encourage those who would like to do a better job of managing that finite resource we call "time."

I commend this book to you with the prayer that you "walk in wisdom . . . redeeming the time" (Col. 4:5, KJV).

You are loved!
Stan Toler
Eph. 3:20-21

# WHAT IS TIME?

❦ Dost thou love life? Then do not squander time, for that is the stuff life is made of.

*Benjamin Franklin*

❦ Time is whatever we want most, but what we use worst.

*William Penn*

❦ Time has no independent existence apart from the order of events by which we measure it.

*Albert Einstein*

❀ Time is merely the order of events, not an entity itself.

*Gottfried Leibniz*

❀ Time: "A . . . continuum that is measured in terms of events which succeed one another from past through present to future."

*Merriam-Webster's Collegiate Dictionary (10th Edition)*

The supply of time is a daily miracle. You wake up in the morning and your purse is magically filled with 24 hours of life. It is yours. It is the most precious of possessions. No one can take it from you. No one receives more or less than you receive. In the realm of time there is no aristocracy of wealth, and no aristocracy of intellect. Genius is not rewarded by even one extra hour a day.

*Arnold Bennett*

Time is a dressmaker specializing in alterations.

*Faith Baldwin*

Time is one of the most important ingredients in any successful formula for any human activity. Invest it wisely.

Time is the father of truth.

*John Florio*

❦ Time is an education for eternity.

❦ Time gives good advice.

*Maltese proverb*

❦ Time is nature's way of keeping everything from happening all at once.

❦ Time is the coin of your life. It is the only coin you have, and only you can determine how it will be spent. Be careful lest you let other people spend it for you.

*Carl Sandburg*

❦ Yesterday is a canceled check; tomorrow is a promissory note; today is the only cash you have—so spend it wisely.

*Kay Lyons*

❤ Time isn't a commodity, something you pass around like cake. Time is the substance for life. When anyone asks you to give your time, they're really asking for a chunk of your life.

*Antoinette Bosco*

❤ Time is one thing we all possess. Our success depends on the proper use of our time and its by-product, the odd moment.

❀ When people say, She's got everything, I've only one answer: I haven't had tomorrow.
*Elizabeth Taylor*

❀ We must use time as a tool, not as a couch.
*John F. Kennedy*

Time is but the stream I go fishing in. I drink it; but while I drink it I see the sandy bottom and detect how shallow it is. Its thin current slides away, but eternity remains.

*Henry David Thoreau*

# THE VALUE OF TIME

Too much to do, too little time. It's everyone's complaint.

You have to live on this twenty-four hours of daily time. Out of it you have to spin wealth, pleasure, money, content, respect, and the evolution of your immortal soul. Its right use is a matter of highest urgency . . . all depends on that.

*Arnold Bennett*

❦ The average person lives 74 years. That is approximately 888 months; 27,010 days; 648,240 hours; 38,894,400 minutes; and 2,022,508,800 heartbeats.

❦ Effective executives, in my observation, do not start with their tasks. They start with their time. They start by finding out where their time goes. Then they attempt to manage their time and to cut back unproductive demands on their time.

*Peter F. Drucker*

✿ Four things come not back: the spoken word, the spent arrow, the past life, and the neglected opportunity.

*Arabian proverb*

✿ Real time management is self-management.

✿ Waste of wealth is sometimes retrieved; waste of health, seldom; but waste of time, never.

Time is an equal opportunity employer. Each human being has exactly the same number of hours and minutes every day. Rich people can't buy more hours. Scientists can't invent new minutes. And you can't save time and spend it on another day. Even so, time is amazingly fair and forgiving. No matter how much time you've wasted in the past, you still have an entire tomorrow. Success depends upon using it wisely by planning and setting priorities. The fact is, time is worth more than money, and by killing time, we are killing our own chances for success.

*Denis Waitley*

Among the aimless, unsuccessful, or worthless, you often hear talk about "killing time." Those who are always killing time are really killing their own chances in life. Those who are destined to become successful are those who make time live by making it useful.

*Arthur Brisbane*

No person will have occasion to complain of the want of time who never loses any.

*Thomas Jefferson*

It has been my observation that most people get ahead during the time that others waste.

*Henry Ford*

The great dividing line between success and failure can be expressed in six words: "I did not have the time."

*Robert J. Hastings*

## God's Minute

I have only just a minute,
Only sixty seconds in it.
Didn't seek it, didn't choose it,
But it's up to me to use it.
I must suffer if I lose it,
Give account if I abuse it.
Just a tiny little minute,
But eternity is in it.

*Rudyard Kipling*

❀ Persistence is the twin sister of excellence. One is a matter of quality; the other, a matter of time.

*Marabel Morgan*

❀ One today is worth two tomorrows.
*Benjamin Franklin*

## He Hadn't Time

He hadn't time to pen a note,
He hadn't time to cast a vote,
He hadn't time to sing a song,
He hadn't time to right a wrong;
He hadn't time to love or give,
He hadn't time to really live.
From now on he'll have time on end—
He died today, my "busy" friend.

*Anonymous*

There are fine things which you mean to do some day, under what you think will be more favorable circumstances. But the only time that is surely yours is the present, hence this is the time to speak the word of appreciation and sympathy, to do the generous deed, to forgive the fault of a thoughtless friend, to sacrifice self a little more for others. Today is the day in which to express your noblest qualities of mind and heart, to do at least one worthy thing which you have long postponed, and to use your God-given abilities for the enrichment of someone less fortunate. Today you can make your life significant and worthwhile. The present is yours to do with as you will.

*Grenville Kleiser*

A sense of the value of time . . . is an essential preliminary to efficient work; it is the only method of avoiding hurry.

*Arnold Bennett*

He that will not apply new remedies must expect new evils; for time is the greatest innovator.

*Francis Bacon*

With time and patience the mulberry leaf becomes a silk gown.

*Chinese proverb*

##  Facts on Time Management

1. We all waste time.
2. We cannot change time.
3. We must accept time as mankind's most important resource.
4. We cannot increase the quantity of time.
5. We cannot do everything.
6. We can only control time.
7. We must accept the fact that we are all procrastinators.

*Antonio Herrera*

The important task must be done today, or even this week. The urgent task calls for instant action. The momentary appeal of these tasks seems irresistible and they devour our energy. But in the light of time's perspective, their deceptive prominence fades. With a sense of loss we recall the important tasks pushed aside. We realize we've become slaves to the tyranny of the urgent.

*Charles E. Hummel*

❦ **If living to be 70 years of age, the average person spends**

- 20 years sleeping
- 20 years working
- 6 years eating
- 7 years playing
- 5 years dressing
- 1 year on the telephone
- 2.5 years in bed
- 3 years waiting for someone
- 6 months tying shoes
- 2.5 years for other things (including 1½ years in church)

In football when the team faces a tough decision, the coach often calls a time-out. In basketball when the press is on, the captain can call for a time-out. In soccer when the team is bushed, they can gain a few minutes' rest with a time-out. But life does not work that way. There is no way we can stop the clock to think about our problems. We cannot save, store, or stretch time. We may use, or we may abuse, time, but the clock keeps on ticking. We can only plan how to spend the time given to us.

*Wayne Rouse*

# TOP 12
# TIME BUSTERS

Make each day useful and cheerful and prove that you know the worth of time by employing it well. Then youth will be happy, elders will be without regret, and life will be a beautiful success.

*Louisa May Alcott*

## 💮 *Time Buster No. 1*
## Busy Work Without Meaning

This is not an instant transformation but a life-long process. As we allow God to reshape our priorities, we will begin to discuss the creative stewardship of time.

*Lawrence Osborne*

### *Time Buster No. 2*
**Inability to Delegate**

The purpose of delegating is to transmit power from a superior to a subordinate so the latter can accomplish a necessary task.

*Ross A. Webber*

### *Time Buster No. 3*
**Putting Things Off**

Procrastination is opportunity's natural assassin.

*Victor Kiam*

❦ Procrastination (of vital tasks) is a close relative of incompetence and a handmaiden of inefficiency.

*Alec Mackenzie*

❦ Procrastination is the thief of time.

*Edward Young*

### ❀ *Time Buster No. 4*
### Unexpected Guests

Don't be defeated by a self-fulfilling prophecy that your interruptions can't be controlled. To control interruptions, analyze the cause; then apply some common sense and a positive attitude.

*Jack D. Ferner*

## ❦ *Time Buster No. 5*
## Pointless Meetings

Questions to ask about all meetings:

1. Why have this meeting?
2. Who should attend this meeting?
3. How should this meeting be organized?
4. How can we maximize our meeting minutes?
5. Should we meet again? If so, how often?

## 🦋 *Time Buster No. 6*
### Poor Preparation

If you haven't got the time to do it right, when will you ever have the time to do it over?

## 🦋 *Time Buster No. 7*
### Habitual Tardiness

There is a trick to avoid being late. Just set your clock 20 minutes ahead, and you'll never be late. Of course, you may get fired for leaving too early.

### 🐝 *Time Buster No. 8*
### Trying to Do Too Much

More people are interested in doing things right than in doing the right things.

*Peter Drucker*

## 🦋 *Time Buster No. 9*
### Telephone Calls

Tips for phone efficiency:

1. Screen all phone calls.
2. Return phone calls in time blocks.
3. Establish phone appointments.
4. Use E-mail or faxes instead of the phone.

### ✿ *Time Buster No. 10*
**A Messy Work Space**

With the elimination of clutter, things become less complicated.

*Milton Mayeroff*

### ✿ *Time Buster No. 11*
**Lack of Planning**

The more time we spend planning a project, the less time is required for it. Do not let today's busy work crowd planning time out of your schedule.

*Edwin Bliss*

### ❦ *Time Buster No. 12*
### Inability to Concentrate

1. Get to meetings early so you can compose yourself before the others arrive.
2. When the phone rings, let it ring one extra time to "get centered."
3. Practice "mindfulness" by doing just one thing at a time, giving it your full attention.
4. Pause after you finish one task before beginning another. If possible, make it last for several minutes.
5. While waiting for a fax or an elevator, think about the present instead of succumbing to the rush and anxiety of tasks still waiting.

*Stephan Rechtschaffen*

# TIME BOOSTERS

• Ask daily, "What is the best use of my time?"
- Save time by asking for help.
- Return phone calls in time blocks.
- Take a 10-minute "power nap" to overcome afternoon drowsiness.
- Throw away junk mail.
- Find a place to work outside the office.
- Carry work with you when going to appointments where possible delays exist.
- Eliminate activities that sap your energy.
- Don't be afraid to say no to time takers!
- Create a system to manage your workload—if all else fails, read the directions!

- Use the tests of time:
    1. The test of necessity
    2. The test of opportunity
    3. The test of efficiency
- Plan to plan:
    1. Write a personal mission statement.
    2. Determine a course of action.
    3. Involve the whole team.
    4. Set a deadline and goals.
    5. Delegate responsibilities to capable teammates.
    6. Review your accomplishments.
- If you fail to control the events in your life, then events in your life will control you.
- Ask a talkative person to give "the short version."

❦ A day is a miniature eternity.

*Ralph Waldo Emerson*

❦ Every bit of time that you save by making it useful or more profitable is that much added to your life and its possibilities. Every minute lost is a neglected product—once gone, you will never get it back.

Think of the odd quarter of an hour before breakfast, the odd half hour after lunch. Remember the chance to read, figure, or think with concentration about your career that presents itself now and again during the day. All these opportunities are the by-products of your daily existence. Use them, and you may find what many successful companies have found —that the real profit is in the utilization of the by-products.

##  Time Bites

1. Clean off the desk.
2. Leave meetings early.
3. Get up 15 minutes early.
4. Delay unnecessary reading.
5. Read only parts of books.
6. Work on the majors only.
7. Make no radical changes.
8. Avoid the wood, hay, and stubble activities.
9. Know any limitations.
10. Ask permission to say no.
11. Schedule work according to productive hours.
12. Discipline self-talk.

## 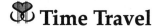 Time Travel

Here are three tips from Philip R. Thomas, author of *Time Warrior,* who logs 250,000 miles each year:

1. Taking baggage onto the plane saves 20 minutes of waiting at baggage claim.
2. Pre-check-in by phone eliminates standing in line at the hotel.
3. To avoid vehicle rental registration lines, pre-hire a limo.

##  Time Management

### Schedule Your Tasks
Stick to a schedule whenever possible, and you will accomplish much in little time. Begin with a written schedule, initially allowing extra time.

### Eliminate the Extraneous
Don't let other tasks interrupt what you are doing; do the secondary tasks later. Rid yourself of distractions, and you will accomplish much more.

## Combine Your Tasks

Typically you can do two or three related tasks at once. These related tasks will be apparent as you see similar activities occurring throughout the day that could be coupled together. For instance, you can handle several errands with the car during one trip.

*Douglas Erlandson*

There are only two kinds of travel: first class and with children.

*Robert Benchley*

❦ We have to live but one day at a time, but we are living for eternity in that one day.

❦ You can't make footprints on the sands of time sitting down.

❦ I recommend that you take care of the minutes, for the hours will take care of themselves.

*Lord Chesterfield*

❦ People who feel good about themselves produce good results.

*Kenneth Blanchard*

# PLANNING TIME
# TO SUCCEED

- Work with a daily "Things to do" list.
- Prioritize daily work assignments.
- Set deadlines for every project file.
- Research a topic thoroughly before acting.
- Divide work into
  Priority 1: "Can't wait"
  Priority 2: "Could wait"
  Priority 3: "Must wait"
- Create a system to manage workload.
- Planning time for God, family, yourself, and others will pay lifelong dividends.
- Buy a time management planner.
- Evaluate your use of time—keep a daily time journal.
- Monitor your performance.

❀ Show me a way to get more things done with my time, and I'll pay you anything within reason.

*Charles Schwab to*
*Ivy Lee*

❀ Write down the most important tasks you have to do tomorrow, and number them in order of importance.

*Ivy Lee to*
*Charles Schwab*

❀ Every minute spent in planning saves ten in execution.

*John Maxwell*

The more rushed we are, the more time we better spend planning our time and actions. Otherwise, we become like the frantic driver who is too much in a hurry to go two miles out of his way to take the freeway; and who then proceeds to burn himself up, rushing, then cussing every red light and every slowpoke on the old highway.

*Stephen Covey*

❧ Since not all tasks are created equal, the organized executive must set priorities: that is, establish a hierarchy of importance, and match the commitment of time and resources to the relative importance of each task.

*Stephanie Winston*

❧ If you really know what things you want out of life, it's amazing how opportunities will come to enable you to carry them out.

*John M. Goddard*

What may be done at any time will be done at no time.

*Scottish proverb*

This time, like all times, is a very good one, if we but know what to do with it.

*Ralph Waldo Emerson*

"Someday" is not a day of the week.

❀ We don't have an eternity to realize our dreams, only the time we are here.

*Susan Taylor*

❀ Since time flies, it's up to you to be the navigator.

# TIME FOR WORK

• Avoid work overload by clarifying job descriptions and expectations with the boss.
- Give clear directions to fellow employees.
- Occasionally close your office door.
- Set goals that reflect the mission of your organization.
- Establish time limits for all meetings.
- As for boring meetings—begin on time, follow an agenda, and establish time limits on speeches.
- Reduce paperwork by empowering someone to open your mail.
- Delegate! Delegate! Delegate!
- Ask for feedback from your team—it will save time, pain, and agony.

I believe you are your work. Don't trade the stuff of your life, time, for nothing more than dollars. That's a rotten bargain.

*Rita Mae Brown*

Great men never complain about the lack of time. Alexander the Great and John Wesley accomplished everything they did in twenty-four-hour days.

*Fred Smith*

The day will happen whether or not you get up.

*John Ciardi*

If you do the things you need to do when you need to do them, then someday you can do the things you want to do when you want to do them.

*Zig Ziglar*

# USING THAT EXTRA TIME WISELY

So much of our time is preparation, so much is routine, and so much retrospect, that the path of each man's genius contracts itself to a very few hours.

*Ralph Waldo Emerson*

##  Time

*Take time to pray*—it helps to bring God near and washes the dust of the earth from your eyes.

*Take time to worship*—it is the highway to reverence.

*Take time for work*—it is the price of success.

*Take time to think*—it is the source of power.

*Take time to play*—it is the secret of youth.

*Take time to read*—it is the foundation of wisdom.

*Take time to be friendly*—it is the road to happiness.

*Take time to dream*—it hitches the soul to the stars.

*Take time to love*—it is the highest joy of life.

*Take time to laugh*—it is the music of the soul.

❧ We need quiet time to examine our lives openly and honestly. . . . Spending quiet time alone gives your mind an opportunity to renew itself and create order.

*Susan Taylor*

❧ The secret of life is enjoying the passage of time.

*James Taylor*

##  The Time Is Now

If you are ever going to love me,
  Love me now, while I can know
The sweet and tender feelings
  From which true affection flow.
Love me now while I am living.
  Do not wait until I'm gone.
And then have it chiseled in marble,
  Sweet words on ice-cold stone.

If you have tender thoughts of me, please tell me now.

If you wait until I am sleeping, never to awaken,

There will be death between us, and I won't hear you then.

So, if you love me, even a little bit, let me know it

While I am living so I can treasure it.

*Author unknown*

❦ Focus 90 percent of your time on solutions and only 10 percent of your time on problems.

*Anthony J. D'Angelo*

❦ Creativity is inventing, experimenting, growing, taking risks, breaking rules, making mistakes, and having fun.

*Mary Lou Cook*

##  Time

What time is it?
Time to do well,
Time to live better,
Give up that grudge,
Answer that letter,
Speak the kind word to sweeten a sorrow,
Do that kind deed you would leave 'til to-
  morrow.

*Anonymous*

❦ The best inheritance a parent can give to his children is a few minutes of his time each day.

*M. Grundler*

❦ Nobody sees a flower really; it is so small. We haven't time, and to see takes time, like to have a friend takes time.

*Georgia O'Keefe*

I would rather be ashes than dust! I would rather that my spark should burn out in a brilliant blaze than it should be stifled by dry-rot. I would rather be a superb meteor, every atom of me in magnificent glow, than a sleepy and permanent planet. The proper function of man is to live, not to exist. I shall not waste my days in trying to prolong them. I shall use my time.

*Jack London*

❦ Nothing is a waste of time if you use the experience wisely.

*Rodin*

❦ One day at a time—this is enough. Do not look back and grieve over the past, for it is gone; and do not be troubled about the future, for it has not yet come. Live in the present and make it so beautiful that it will be worth remembering.

*Ida Scott Taylor*

# SIGNS OF THE TIMES

❀ The clock represents our commitments, appointments, schedules, goals, activities—what we do with, and how we manage our time.

*Stephen R. Covey*

**Store clock display:** There's no present like time.

**Sign over classroom clock:** Time will pass. Will you?

**Sign on office communication board:** In case of fire, don't panic. Simply leave the building with the same reckless abandon that occurs each day at quitting time.

**Sign of the times:** If you think time heals everything, try waiting in a doctor's office.

**Factory sign:** If you have nothing to do, please don't do it here.

**Sundial inscription:** It is later than you think.

I must govern the clock, not be governed by it.

*Golda Meir*

# TIME TO SMILE

❀ I am definitely going to take a course in time management . . . just as soon as I can work it into my schedule.

*Louis E. Boone*

❀ People count the faults of those who keep them waiting.

*French proverb*

##  The Procrastinator's Poem

I've gone for a drink and sharpened my pencils,
Searched through my desk for forgotten utensils.
I reset my watch, I adjusted my chair,
I've loosened my tie and straightened my hair.
I filled my pen and tested the blotter
And gone for another drink of water.
Adjusted the calendar, and I've raised the blind,
And I've sorted erasers of all different kinds.
Now down to work I can finally sit.
Oops, it's too late. It's time to quit.

## 🏵 Too Late

The story is told of a man who rushed into a suburban railroad station one morning and almost breathlessly asked the ticket agent, "When does the 8:01 leave?"

"At 8:01" was the answer.

"Well," the man replied, "it's 7:59 by my watch, 7:57 by the town clock, and 8:04 by the station clock. Which am I to go by?"

"You can go by any clock you wish," said the agent. "But you can't go by the 8:01 train—it's already left."

## 🕮 What Time Is It?

A man from the city driving through a small mountain town screeched to a halt and shouted to an old-timer sitting on a bench: "Hey, what time is it?"

"Twelve o'clock," replied the old man.

"Are you sure?" the driver snapped. "I thought it was later than that."

"Don't never get no later than that around here," drawled the old man. "When it gets to twelve, we start all over."

## 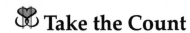 Take the Count

A prizefighter, having a rough time in his first important fight, was floored in the second round by a powerful punch. With glazed eyes, he tried to look up from the mat.

"Let the referee count," yelled his trainer. "Don't get up until eight!"

The fighter nodded and weakly replied, "What time is it now?"

John Kennedy used to tell about a famous French marshal who once asked his gardener to plant a tree. The gardener objected that the tree was growing too slowly and would not reach maturity for 100 years. The marshal replied, "In that case there's no time to lose—plant it this afternoon."

The longest wait in the world is when the nurse tells you to take off your clothes and the doctor will be with you in a moment.

When a man sits with a pretty girl for an hour, it seems like a minute. But let him sit on a hot stove for a minute, and it's longer than any hour. That's relativity.

*Albert Einstein*

Time is a great teacher, but unfortunately it kills all its pupils.

*Hector Berlioz*

A patient who had survived a serious accident asked his doctor, "Doc, how long will I have to lie here?"
Wisely, his doctor replied, "Only one day at a time."

Mr. Meant-to has a comrade
   And his name is Didn't-do.
Have you ever chanced to meet them?
   Did they ever call on you?
These two fellows live together
   In the house of Never-win
And I'm told that it is haunted
   By the ghost of Might-have-been.

*Samuel Johnson*

❦ My evening visitors, if they cannot see the clock, should find the time in my face.

*Ralph Waldo Emerson*

❦ I have noticed that the people who are late are often so much jollier than the people who have to wait for them.

*E. V. Lucas*

❦ A person with an hour to kill usually wants to spend it with someone who can't spare a minute.

# TIME FOR
# INSPIRATION

A thousand years in your sight are like a day that has just gone by, or like a watch in the night.

*Ps. 90:4*

Be very careful, then, how you live—not as unwise but as wise, making the most of every opportunity, because the days are evil.

*Eph. 5:15-16*

Teach us to number our days aright, that we may gain a heart of wisdom.

*Ps. 90:12*

He who works his land will have abundant food, but he who chases fantasies lacks judgment.

*Prov. 12:11*

Time wasted is a theft from God.
*Henri Frederic Amiel*

I have so much to do today that I shall spend the first three hours in prayer.
*Martin Luther*

God has given me this day to use as I will. I can waste it, or use it for good, but what I do today is important because I am exchanging a day of my life for it.

*Heartsill Wilson*

God gave you the gift of 86,400 seconds today. Have you used one to say "thank You"?

*William A. Ward*

Time and tide wait for no man.

*Proverb*

##  Slow Me Down, Lord!

Slow me down, Lord!
Ease the pounding of my heart by the quieting of my
    mind.
Steady my hurried pace
With a vision of the eternal reach of time.
Give me, amidst the confusion of my day,
The calmness of the everlasting hills.
Break the tension of my nerves
With the soothing music of the singing streams
That live in my memory.
Help me to know the magical restoring power of sleep.

Teach me the art of taking minute vacations, of slow-
   ing down to look at a flower,
To chat with an old friend or make a new one,
To pat a stray dog, to watch a spider build a web,
To smile at a child, or to read from a good book.
Remind me each day
That the race is not always to the swift,
That there is more to life than increasing its speed.
Let me look upward into the towering oak
And know that it is great and strong
Because it grew slowly and well.

Orin L. Crain

❧ When God wants to grow a squash, He grows it in one summer; but when He wants to grow an oak, He takes a century.

*James A. Garfield*

❧ Let the year be given to God in its every moment! The year is made up of minutes: let these be watched as having been dedicated to God! It is in the sanctification of the small that hallowing of the large is secure.

*G. Campbell Morgan*

❀ We will have all eternity to celebrate the victories, but only a few hours before sunset to win them.

*Amy Carmichael*

❀ It's only when we truly know and understand that we have a limited time on earth—and that we have no way of knowing when our time is up—that we will begin to live each day to the fullest, as if it was the only one we had.

*Elisabeth Kubler-Ross*

# TIMELESS WORDS

Though I am always in haste, I am never in a hurry; because I never undertake any more work than I can go through with perfect calmness of spirit.

*John Wesley*

Time is everything. Please act in view of this.

*Abraham Lincoln*
*to Union governors*
*July 3, 1862*

Time does not become sacred to us until we have lived it.

*John Burroughs*

❀ Life is no brief candle to me. It's a sort of splendid torch which I've got to hold up for the moment and I want to make it burn as brightly as possible before handing it on to future generations.

*George Bernard Shaw*

❀ The time is always right to do what is right.
*Martin Luther King Jr.*

❀ As if you could kill time without injuring eternity.
*Henry David Thoreau,*
Walden

❀ We are what we repeatedly do. Excellence, then, is not an act, but a habit.

*Aristotle*

❀ Lives of great men all remind us
    We can make our lives sublime,
And, departing, leave behind us
    Footprints on the sands of time.

*Henry Wadsworth Longfellow,*
A Psalm of Life

❀ There is no mortar that time will not loose.

*French proverb*

❀ Nothing gives so much direction to a person's life as a set of sound principles.

*Ralph Waldo Emerson*

❀ Time is the nurse and breeder of all good.

*William Shakespeare*

❀ Write it on your heart that every day is the best day in the year.

*Ralph Waldo Emerson*

If one advances confidently in the direction of his dreams, and endeavors to live the life which he has imagined, he will meet with a success unexpected in common hours.

*Henry David Thoreau,*
Walden

Everything comes to him who hustles while he waits.

*Thomas Edison*

Every morning we have 86,400 seconds before us to spend and to invest. Each day the bank named "time" opens a new account. It allows no balances. No overdrafts. If we fail to use the day's deposits, the loss is ours.

*Billy Graham*

There's a time for some things, and a time for all things; a time for great things, and a time for small things.

*Cervantes,*
Don Quixote

❦ Comedy is tragedy plus time.

*Carol Burnett*

❦ Time as he grows old teaches many lessons.

*Aeschylus*

❦ Habits are like a cable. We weave a strand of it every day, and soon it cannot be broken.

*Horace Mann*

❀ Look not mournfully into the Past. It comes not back again. Wisely improve the Present. It is thine. Go forth to meet the shadowy Future, without fear, and with a manly heart.

*Henry Wadsworth Longfellow,*
Hyperion

❀ Future—that period of time in which our affairs prosper, our friends are true and our happiness is assured.

*Ambrose Bierce*

❀ The reason so many people never get anywhere in life is because when opportunity knocks, they are out in the backyard looking for four-leaf clovers.

*Walter P. Chrysler*

❀ Guard well your spare moments. They are like uncut diamonds. Discard them and their value will never be known. Improve them and they will become the brightest gems in a useful life.

*Ralph Waldo Emerson*

**Time**

Time rides with the old
At a great pace. As travelers on swift steeds
See the near landscape fly and flow behind them,
While the remoter fields and dim horizons
Go with them, and seem wheeling round to
   meet them,
So in old age things near us slip away,
And distant things go with us.

*Henry Wadsworth Longfellow*

To every thing there is a season, and a time to every purpose under the heaven: A time to be born, and a time to die; a time to plant, and a time to pluck up that which is planted; a time to kill, and a time to heal; a time to break down, and a time to build up; a time to weep, and a time to laugh; a time to mourn, and a time to dance; a time to cast away stones, and a time to gather stones together; a time to embrace, and a time to refrain from embracing; a time to get, and a time to lose; a time to keep, and a time to cast away; a time to rend, and a time to sew; a time to keep silence, and a time to speak; a time to love, and a time to hate; a time of war, and a time of peace.

*Eccles. 3:1-8, KJV*